A Gift For:

....

From:

....

Published by Hallmark Gift Books,
a division of Hallmark Cards, Inc.,
Kansas City, MO 64141
Visit us on the Web at Hallmark.com.

Editorial Director: Delia Berrigan
Editors: Lee Stuart and Dan Taylor
Art Director: Chris Opheim
Designer: Scott Swanson
Production Designer: Dan Horton

ISBN: 978-1-63059-982-9
1BOK2278

Made in China
1117

Chapter 1

"I'M NOT TAKING CREDIT SO MUCH AS DENYING RESPONSIBILITY."

When Hallmark launched Shoebox in 1986, nobody knew that the crabby character gracing the covers of a few Shoebox cards would become a celebrity. But it didn't take long to see that Maxine's irreverent quips about aging, the workplace, retirement, political correctness, and of course sex (or the lack of it) had struck a chord.

Since then, Americans have purchased hundreds of millions of Maxine greeting cards, and Maxine is still the first and only greeting card character to move from the card aisle into popular culture.

As Hallmark's top-performing character, today Maxine has her own books, comic strip, calendars, and Facebook page. Her likeness—and attitude—have also appeared on everything from T-shirts to paper towels.

John Wagner—or "Arty-Boy," as Maxine likes to call him—says Maxine was inspired by his mother, his maiden aunts, and his grandmother. John remembers doodling as a preschooler, and says both his mother and his grandmother encouraged his artistic interests. He eventually attended the Vesper George School of Art in Boston, after which he landed at Hallmark as part of a new artist group.

It was the birth of the humorous Shoebox Greetings (a tiny little division of Hallmark) in 1986 that added a new dimension to John's professional life. The Shoebox way of seeing the world unleashed his talents, and he began to draw Maxine.

"Cartoonists are sensitive to the insanities of the world," John says. "If Maxine can get a laugh out of someone who feels lonely or someone who is getting older and hates the thought of another birthday, or if she can make someone chuckle about stressful interpersonal relationships, then I'm happy. Putting a smile on someone's face is what it's all about."

Those smiles have led to Maxine becoming a bit of a celebrity. Fans nationwide collect Maxine items. Letters to John and Maxine reveal that fans feel a very personal connection to the character, with many insisting they (or a relative) are "just like Maxine."

Many also wonder . . . how did she get that name? "People at Shoebox started referring to the character as 'John Wagner's old lady,' and I knew that would get me into trouble with my wife," John says. The Shoebox team had a contest amongst themselves to name the character, and three of the approximately 30 entries suggested "Maxine," making the name the clear winner.

Let's look at each of the decades since Maxine took over the world to see what she's done with it. Hold on to your bunny slippers; it's gonna be a crabby ride!

Chapter 2
The 1980s

"OR AS I CALL IT, THE DECADE OF LIKE, TOTALLY, ANNOYING HAIRDOS."

John Wagner, Creator

John's Mom, Toni

"The 1980s, an entire decade that's mostly remembered for shoulder pads. I remember it as a magical time full of unicorns and leprechauns, but that might be because I inhaled a lot of hairspray. The 80s were where I really began to take off. Get your minds out of the gutter! I meant 'became more popular.'"

Getting my knee tapped with that little hammer is a great excuse to kick the doctor in the shins!

Life is what you make it.
I make it unbearable
for as many people
as possible.

Looking on the bright side hurts my eyes.

Chapter 3
The 1990s

"SHOPPING IN MY PAJAMAS. NOT ONLINE, JUST WEARING PAJAMAS."

Shoebox Team Circa 90s-ish?

"You can't talk about the 90s without mentioning the Internet explosion. Which was the time I got so mad at my dial-up computer that I stuffed it full of firecrackers and blew the motherboard.com out of it."

If you stay away from alcohol, sex, and fried food, you still won't live forever... but it sure will feel like it!

They say walking is the best exercise. They say so many things...

JWagner

I believe that no problem is too large or too difficult to be blamed on someone else.

If those Terminator movies have taught me anything, it's that hybrid technology is risky business.
JWagner

When I call it a
"Girls Night Out,"
what I mean is
that I'm not going
to wear a bra.

JWagner

CENSORED!!

I'm looking for the same thing as a lot of attractive single men... an attractive single man!

JWagner

John and Maxine

"The 2000s! A decade of flying cars and drive-through plastic surgery for everyone! Or, another time the guys who predict the future proved they can't predict the future. Yeah, I think it's that second one."

I tell everyone, "If you're ever in trouble, call me!" Yeah, I love hearing about other people in trouble.
JWagner

John with a flock of Maxines

"The 2010s have proven to be everything you dreamed if you dreamed they wouldn't be much. There's still not a flying car hovering above your garage, and last I checked there was no foot-rubbin' robot giving my feet a good going-over. The good news, apparently, is that there's still plenty, and I mean plenty, to complain about."

The good news is my mind still wanders to sex. The bad news is now it uses a walker.

They say you need to listen to what your body is telling you... but mine just points and laughs.

JWagner

We have very predictable weather where I work. Every morning, a strong, stupid front moves in.
I ♥ MY ATTITUDE PROBLEM
JWagner

Boy, after putting in seven or eight hours of work, I'm ready to call it a week.
JWagner

I have no problem with friends asking to borrow money. I love a good laugh as much as anyone.

I miss the days when you could slam down your phone without it costing you $300.

If at first you don't succeed... you probably had a man helping you.
JWagner

Maxine

"Time passes. This is something I have to remind myself after a big meal, but it's got a positive side, too. While the future is as unpredictable as a squirrel in the middle of the street, there are a few things coming up that almost make it worth getting out of bed in the morning."

All you have to do is sit back and let Maxine keep bringing the crabby. Don't worry; she's nowhere close to running out, and as long as you're laughing, the hits will keep on comin'!

A centerfold's not that big a deal. Heck, I've got folds everywhere.

Maxine and her adoring fans have been on a wild ride, and it's just getting started! There are all kinds of new things in the works, some we can tell you about and some you'll just have to wait and see. But one of the biggest, newest, singin-gest, dancingest, scary ghostyest things will be Maxine's Christmas Carol! It will debut in Branson, Missouri, and then who knows where it'll go! Make plans now to see Maxine live on stage!

If you were bored enough to read this book and it made you happy, we don't think there's much we can do for you. But we'd love to hear from you, anyway.

Please send comments to:
Hallmark Book Feedback
P.O. Box 419034
Mail Drop 100
Kansas City, MO 64141

Or email us at:
booknotes@hallmark.com